The Raid of the Grackles and Other Poems

John D. Groppe

Cover design by Beth Bassett, Brook, IN

The Raid of the Grackles and Other Poems

ISBN-13:
978-0692765999 (Iroquois River Press)

ISBN-10:
0692765999

The Iroquois River Press
711 E Grace Street
Rensselaer, IN 47978

To Rose Marie
my primary inspiration,
and our children and their partners and spouses
and our grandchildren,
our most important creation

I also wish to acknowledge
my indebtedness and gratitude
to my friends and colleagues
of the Prairie Writers Guild
of Rensselaer, Indiana,
without whose enthusiasm for writing
and encouragement of my efforts
this book would not be in your hands.

Acknowledgments

The following poems were published in *From The Edge of the Prairie* (Prairie Writers Guild, Rensselaer, IN): "Before Dawn," "February," "Spring Plowing," 2004; "Just So, a Poem," "The Raid of the Grackles," 2005; "Singing with the Pleiades" and "The Work of Spring," 2007; "Instincts of Grace," "My Grandparents' Land: Killaloe, County Clare, Ireland," "On a Pen and Ink Sketch of a Morel," 2013; "On Adam Vanderwielen's *Community*," "When the Soldiers Came," 2014; "I Am Still Here," "Snagged Words," "The Nighthawks," 2015; "The Artist's Paint Tray," "Force Suspended," "More You Than Me," 2016.

The following poems were published in the *Tipton Poetry Journal* (Zionsville, IN): "February," Winter, 2008; "Singing with the Pleiades," Spring, 2010; "On a Pen and Ink Sketch of a Morel," Winter-Spring, 2013; and "When the Soldiers Came," 2016.

The following poems were published in *Through the Sycamores* (http://www.throughthesycamores.com/), "The Bird Etched in Stone," "Spring Plowing," 2016.

"The Raid of the Grackles" was published in the Indiana Humanities Council on line celebration of National Poetry Month, April 16, 2012 (http://indianahumanities.org/april-16-the-raid-of-the-grackles-by-john-d-groppe).

"My Grandparents' Land: Killaloe, County Clare, Ireland" was selected for presentation at The Borderlands Poetry Project north reading, University of Notre Dame, Mar. 27, 2013.

"A Fear Too Great" was published in *Flying Island* (Writers Center of Indianapolis), Winter-Spring, 1990.

"Word Winger: A Self Portrait" was published in *Skylark* (Purdue University Northwest) Spring, 1983.

"The Word That Comes" was published in *Interdisciplinary Perspectives*, Fall 1981.

Mr. Groppe was listed on Indiana's bicentennial literary map *1816-2016 Literary Map of Indiana: 200 Years-200 Writers*, published by the Indiana State Library in partnership with the Eugene & Marilyn Glick Indiana Authors Award (http://www.in.gov/library/files/1816-2016_Literary_Map_of_Indiana.pdf).

Illustrations

The grackle sketches were drawn by Judith Anne Kanne and used by permission.

The Artist's Paint Tray by Doris Myers was reprinted by permission and was previously published in *From the Edge of the Prairie*, 2016.

Community by Adam Vanderwielan was reprinted by permission and was previously published in *From the Edge of the Prairie*, 2014.

Fisher Oak Savanna photo by John D. Groppe was previously published in *From the Edge of the Prairie*, 2016.

The Icy River by Gordon Quinlan was printed by permission.

John D. Groppe, photo by Jose Arteaga and used by permission.

Morel by Joseph Cross was reprinted by permission and was previously published in *From the Edge of the Prairie*, 2014.

The Nighthawks: Homage to Edward Hopper was previously published in *From the Edge of the Prairie*, 2015.

Passenger Pigeon, Pine Hills Nature Preserve by Shari Wagner was reprinted by permission and was previously published in *Through the Sycamores*, 2016.

The Raid of the Grackles and Other Poems Index

Acknowledgments	
Dedication	
Just So, a Poem	1
Creation and Creativity	2
Winter Storm	3
A Fear Too Great	4
February	5
Spring Plowing	6
The Work of Spring	7
On a Pen and Ink Sketch of a Morel	9
Spring Storm	10
The Raid of the Grackles	11
Singing with the Pleiades	12
My Grandparents' Land—Killaloe, County Clare, Ireland	13
Papa	14
Sheltering Rock: An Honorarium to Sr. Catherine Fay, BVM	15
The Artist's Paint Tray	17
Fear of Failure	18
The Old King Comes	19
Force Suspended: On a Photo by Gordon Quinlan	20
When the Soldiers Came	22
Picking Up Rocks	23
The Bird Carved in Stone	25
Potawatomi Park on the Iroquois River, Jasper County	26
Lovers Like the Sun or Water	27
I Am Still Here	28
Snagged Words	29
Before Dawn	30
The Uptight Jay	31
The Nighthawks	32
Instincts of Grace	33
Earth and Rain	34
More You Than Me	35
On Adam Vanderwielen's *Community*	37
The Word That Comes	38
Word Winger: A Self Portrait	39
About the Author	41

Illustrations

Grackles, pen and ink sketches by Judith Anne Kanne	covers
Fisher Oak Savanna, photo by John D. Groppe	2
Morel, pen and ink sketch by Joseph Cross	8
Killaloe, Ireland, photo by John D. Groppe	13
The Artist's Paint Tray, acrylic by Doris Myers	16
The Icy River, photo by Gordon Quinlan	21
Passenger Pigeon, Pine Hills Nature Preserve, photo by Shari Wagner	24
The Nighthawks 2015: Homage to Edward Hopper, photo by John D. Groppe	32
Community, acrylic by Adam Vanderwielan	36
John D. Groppe, photo by Jose Arteaga	41

Just So, a Poem

Cruing to each other, the cranes
pull deep sweeps on their long wings
like a longboat crew
in disciplined energy and for the joy of it,
each mounting or sidling invisible obstacles
but holding the form until they circle
their intended rest,
and with wings billowed above them
land lightly,
then stand in silence;
just so, a poem—
its words and lines speaking to each other,
following their own reflections,
gathering impressions and for the joy of it,
breaking loose yet keeping the form—
soars to its intended close,
ends in awesome silence.

Creation and Creativity
Fisher Oak Savanna, **photo by John D. Groppe**

We did not plant the trees
in the woods where we love to walk.
We did not plant *les fleurs savauges*
that bedazzle Les Prairies.
We did not nurse the monarchs
or nut hatches or crickets,
the owls and voles
we have seen and heard.
We artists accept these gifts joyfully
and joyfully offer our gifts
of paintings, collages and poems
to those who were not with us
in the woods, savannas, or fields
so they too can know
their own gifts of creation and creativity.

Winter Storm

The north wind twisted icicles
into bayonets and stilettos,
and choked the sun,
and iced the wind chimes into silence.
After dark the snow began.
The northwest corner of the lawn was swept clean
and the driveway buried.
A weary sun discovered trackless drifts
and a dumb world burdened with frost.
But then the birds came back—
first the upside down nuthatches
chipping warily in the elm,
then snowbirds whistling from the low bushes
to the feeder,
a gang of raucous starlings,
chittering sparrows,
a pair of chuckling cardinals.

A Fear Too Great

A flutter in the eaves trough, the wind dead
for a moment, alarmed the girl. "A bird
is stuck," she told me. "Help it," she begged.
I smiled with foolish confidence and fetched
a ladder. The wind, now risen, muted
my clamor, and I came upon the bird
by surprise, a house sparrow, its right foot
frozen to the ice in the trough. Its fear
extended body drew back as if to lift
the trough or snap the leg. I withdrew
quickly and listened to the wind raging
across the open ground, my confidence
gone. I found a screwdriver and, mounting
the ladder, sheltered the bird in my hand,
picked at the ice, broke off a large chunk
and felt the bird die in my grip, go still
like a milliner's thing of straw and wire
and plastic feathers. The wind mocking me,
the bird's foot still ice ringed,
I brought the dead bird down,
stunned at a fear too great for the body.

February

Lending his fire to the setting sun,
a cardinal in a budded magnolia
hastens the snow.
Warmed by his flame,
I vision a mist of star flowers
across the grass in the oak grove
and a wren in the forsythia.
Orange melting across the sky,
the earth tilts toward the sun.

Spring Plowing

The snow being gone
except in the shadows of fence posts,
the glinting discs
open the earth
to the sun and the grackles.

The Work of Spring

The work of spring—the proclaiming, announcing,
desiring, celebrating—is done to music.
Calliopes of sandhill cranes high over head
lead parades of returning performers.
Honking in quick time, Bersaglieri bands of geese
make their way to lakes and ponds.
Each morning, the dark sky yet to be broken,
robins flute in trees impatient for the full chorus to resume.
Ocarina mourning doves coo the days into warmth
while cardinals whistle on the highest branches.
House finches and song sparrows gathering at the feeder
practice their glissandos.
Grackles, adding their bad amp guitar squawks, strut,
heads high, backs arched, like drum majors.
The jays' clarinets and the crows' cawing trumpets
jazz the warming days.
Last to come are the piccolo wrens,
the coloratura warblers, the percussionists—
flickers and red headed woodpeckers.
The work of spring—building, reviving,
defending, rejoicing—is done in polyphony
that glides into diminuendo by summer.
Then the musicians leave silently
except the cranes and the Bersaglieri geese
parading loudly south before the snows.

Morel, pen and ink sketch by Joseph Cross

On a Pen and Ink Sketch of a Morel

Stark, yet alive,
a pen and ink morel emerging
from its cream parchment,
from the blankness of creation,
against black scratches suggesting
the darkness that nurtured
the spore of its being,
its ridges extending,
its dark recesses deepening and darkening,
its head engorging with sweetness
having thrust through the dark earth of its birth
as if in response to some cosmic command—
"Let there be a morel,"
and so it was, and it was good,
and so we rested in the cosmos.

Spring Storm

A lilac night beneath the stirring storm—
the wind filled the air with elm seeds and purple.
Tumbling clouds buried the moon,
and the rain fell.
Lightnings showed the lilacs heavy with water.
The rain fell, and slowed, and fell again.
Four days of rain tore away lilac corollas
and from a cedar branch a robin's nest
with three April hatchlings.
The rain swelled the river
and drowned new corn,
but left the grass tall and thick
with seed where starlings pecked,
and green ponds where grackles bathed,
and, out beyond the lilac,
the spirea burgeoning with white.
Snowbushes, the ruby child called them,
and put a branch in her heart's vase.

The Raid of the Grackles

In the morning the grackles come as shadows
skimming the grass like manta rays
along the ocean floor, then rise
into the cherry tree dimming its brightness,
perch above the feeder, stretch their bodies,
curving them into a U.
One leaps to the feeder, making it spin,
riding it, feeding as he turns,
his talons choking its rim.
Dropping to the ground, his gang stabs
the thick grass for seeds scattered by their leader
and preen in the early sunlight,
flashing iridescent greens and blues.
At a silent signal they go without stealth.
Then sparrows come, finches, a cardinal,
all sharing the wobbling feeder.
The cherry blossoms regain their soft brilliance.

Singing with the Pleiades

Venus is aloof from the Moon in my April sky
while Orion laughs, having learned such wisdom
from his loss of the Seven Sisters of the Pleiades
when they were changed into doves,
and meanwhile those Sisters have begun
their descent below the west
and on the wind I hear them singing
as they leave our skies till the frost returns.
The Mohegans, singing with them,
would begin to plant their corn.
In the morning I go humming to the garage
for my hoe and shovel and seeds.

Killaloe, Ireland, photo by John D. Groppe

My Grandparents' Land—Killaloe, County Clare, Ireland

Too little space between river and hills
to bury all born here,
too little hope here
despite tales of royal glory and the rich river,
so they left and were buried
far from the stone slab huts of hermit monks
and defiant towers of warrior architects,
far from sheepfolds and salmon runs,
and carried with them names from their past
to endow their children
and their children's children
with a kindly courage.

Papa

Papa, twice a widower, loved sunny rooms—
the dining room with his rocking chair
and smoking stand near the window,
and the kitchen with a white wood table
where he served me grapefruit
scraped clean into a bowl
and oatmeal—stir-about he called it—
running with Karo syrup.
Outside he sat on the low stonewall
of Saint James Church on Seventh Avenue
with Walsh, another widower
and Irishman from Clare,
both far from home.
They puffed their pipes, occasionally chuckling
about some bloke who had done a foolish thing.
I sat with them, watching the trolleys
and women pushing baby carriages
while towing toddlers behind
and learned the warmth of the sun,
the delight of a quiet chuckle,
the strength of silence.

**Sheltering Rock: An Honorarium
to Catherine Fay, B.V.M.**

Adamant in her love for those in need,
firm in her resistance to those
lacking the courage of our earthiness
revealed when shared by Mary's son
is Catherine.
It is upon such rocks as these
that the fishermen's friend built his church
as a place where all—children all—
come to be fed and to sing and dance.
She is like the granite arms of Ireland,
resisting the winds and the waves,
embracing her bays,
guiding the sailors home,
rocks flecked with mica to catch the glory of the sun,
rocks that shelter the sea birds—
the terns, shearwaters, and gannets.

The Artist's Paint Tray, acrylic by Doris Myers

The Artist's Paint Tray

My farmscape on the wall there—
a study of violet, white, and green—
was here in this tray, waiting in these tubes.
Mixed, they are fluid—
flowing, brightening, diminishing.
See, the sky is white underneath
with an overlay of violet—mauve really—
and some washes of salmon.
The leaves of the trees flow
from lavender to iris to orchid,
each depending on the white.
The leaves are softer close to the window,
brighter deeper in to draw your eye
to and beyond the bed sheets floating on the breeze
to the resting, expectant barns deep within.
You did not get distracted by the sheets
because of the mauve blushes on the sheets.
Then there's the green of the lawn
with some yellow for brightness
and plum for shade.
The window frames in the foreground—
we look through them, almost ignore them—
are black with some red,
garnet perhaps, or something darker.
All these colors change before you can name them.
Still they do bring you deeper
through the window, across the lawn,
from the dark to the brightened to the bright,
and there, between the white barn
with a periwinkle roof and the brick dust barn,
is the red barn shining forth—just red—
and the white fence in front of it—just white.
You see the farmscape through the window,
but the colors enticed you to enter.

Fear of Failure

She made me feel I was a prince.
though not of royal blood.
I thought her a princess and was enamored
but had nothing to offer
but what she thought she saw
in our laughter, our excursions,
our brief escapes from the limits of our lives.
Yet, in spite of our mute dreams
and out of fear of failure
that what I would offer would be a bare table,
a troubled bed, pawned dreams,
I turned away, still aching—
having failed in trying to avoid failure.

The Old King Comes

Quiet! Hush, dog! There, stop now.
It's the old king.
See how the dog growls and cowers.
The dogs know he's coming.
You'll hear his stick tapping the street stones.
Listen. There. Hear it?
Come here, dog. Quiet now.
I've seen dogs like that only once.
A sick wolf came to the village,
and the dogs were compelled to attack,
to drive him off, but they could smell his evil
and hung back, growling and cowering,
afraid to do what they had been bred to do,
what dogs have always had to do.
They knew the evil would catch them too
and they'd be driven from the village
to survive only on what they could scavenge
and all would fear contagion.
Yes, it's the old king come to feel the civility
he's lost by some god's curse.
When the dogs moan, we bar our doors and shutters
and listen to the dark. Hear him?
He goes to the market and sits in silence
where once he ruled.
It was not his fault. What could he do?
He had been away so long,
how could he know his father or his mother?
Some god long before had cursed them all.
Things have not been so bad for us
since he stabbed his eyes
and went off to the caves by the river.
The wheat and olives and grapes are plenty now,
and we do leave him some outside our doors,
but burn the baskets in the morning.
I suppose you ought to pity an innocent man,
but he should never have come to Thebes.
What had we done
that he should seek warmth from our stones
while we hide in the darkness like the dogs?

Force Suspended: On a Photo by Gordon Quinlan

The river has been halted,
its energy suspended,
held in reserve,
its crushing torrent,
its eroding, propellant force.
The river has been silenced,
its tumult,
its roar,
its sprayed splash,
its lapping waves against the bank.
Here, far from the snowmelt
above the tree line where it was spawned
in droplets freed by the sun
and far from the wide slow rivers
that will carry its energy to the ocean,
we are silenced and stilled,
hesitant to move at this moment
of withheld power,
and we feel what the physicists felt
in the squash court under Stagg Field
when Fermi ordered the last control rod
withdrawn another twelve inches
beyond its already seven foot extension
and the neutron counter clicked with rage—
the neutrons doubling every two minutes—
and Fermi said, "It has gone critical,"
and, pleased with his calculations, grinned
and let the neutrons multiply for almost five minutes
as the others stood in silence,
then ordered the Zip safety rod replaced.
The energy was stopped,
the neutron counter silenced,
the force suspended
but all knew the suspension would not hold.
.

The Icy River, photo by Gordon Quinlan

When the Soldiers Came

When the solders went east,
they praised our farm,
said it was an honor to the fatherland,
and blessed me left shoulder to right.
When they came back, bandaged, limping
in twos and threes, cursing,
they hated our farm, me, my family
and, even though we fed them,
would have shot us if they had the time.

When the soldiers came from the east,
they praised our farm,
said it was a joy to the motherland,
praised us since we could speak their language
without hint of accent
and blessed me right shoulder to left.
When they shambled east,
bandaged, limping, abandoning stragglers—
my wife and children and all
but one son frightened and hiding—
they pissed in our kitchen,
shot what cattle I could not hide
and left them rotting in the sun
and straggled on.

I don't know when to bring forth my family,
when to plant a new crop,
when to feed the lambs from what little we have.
My son and I watch both horizons—
he now with a rifle some soldier dropped—
but I fear some partisans
will come and ask what side we are on.

Picking Up Rocks

You pick up a rock
and a micro world scurries out
in its diversity and small scale energy.
It runs amok and grows in anger,
then hides and waits.
It had made do, had held on.
It did not thrive, but it had held on.
Now it hides and waits.
You replace the rock—
there is no point in holding it—
and in time that world coheres.
But if you pick up a larger rock,
sects, parties, Bunds, clans, vigilantes scurry,
their anger multiplying.
There is no point in replacing the rock.
The fear and anger is implacable
and will have its will.

Passenger Pigeon, Pine Hills Nature Preserve, photo Shari Wagner

The Bird Carved in Stone

Look, there, that flat rock a lighter brown
than the humus rich soil around,
we near missed it almost level with the ground,
and see the outline of a plump bird
carefully etched in the soft, brown stone
with a harder sharp rock—
a passenger pigeon like those that thronged
these skies, a thousands fold clamorous flock.
They are long since gone
as is the man who made this art.
No one scratched his likeness in stone—
his people corralled, their villages burnt—
but in this grove they left a sign, this alone.
Now we must incise this image on our souls
to remember not just the birds killed
in a sport requiring no skill
but also the peoples of this woodland
exiled and scattered
and as silent as this bird.

Potawatomi Park on the Iroquois River, Jasper County

Potawatomi once dwelt here,
hunted the high ground woodlands,
fished the wetlands and the creek
we call a river,
bent trees to mark a trail
to settlements and welcome,
and left arrowheads that emerge
from the sandy soil after a rain.
Crying their way to Kansas,
they left under armed guards
and an act of Congress.
We wanted their forests,
even the great swamp,
for our cattle and corn
and the rivers for sport and trade.
We axed the forests,
drained the great swamp
after slaughtering the water birds for play,
and secured our women, children, and creeds.
The bones of the Potawatomi
do not surface after a rain,
but we have named a park for them
and felt no guilt.

Lovers Like the Sun or Water

I walk this beach, holding the white
billowing skirt against my thighs,
to know the deep cool of water on my feet.
I feel my body—thighs, buttocks, breasts—
full and free under flowing cloth,
and know my own silhouette against the sun.
Why can't the world know me as the water,
as this dress and sun know me?
As I know myself?
Why do the women stiffen and watch their men
when I enter a room?
Did I offend them because I knew
another man besides my husband?
Do I offend them now that I have no lover or husband?
The water soothes my ankles, calves, thighs,
and I pull the dress tighter to wade deeper,
here where there are no angry women, no hungry men,
but why are there no lovers like the sun or water?

I Am Still Here

I am still here
no farther away than always,
but sounds come to me
as if from afar
like voices across a lake,
a conversation in another room,
murmurs down at the end of the bar
late in the evening.
I hear voices like mouse sounds
but without the acuity of mouse ears.
Even in a room alive with voices,
I am more alone with my own silent voices
and have to be called back
from those conversations
to attend to the live voices around me.
I am still here.

Snagged Words

I see the words I want to say—
the opening phrases
almost as a script—
with confidence of what's to follow,
a reply, a clarification,
a distinction or rebuttal,
but like an audio tape snagged
on a cog in the recorder,
I jam on a word,
stumble on a syllable—
the vision of the script dispersed—
and when my tongue rolls again,
I am uncertain as to where to start
and worry about the patience of my hearers.

Before Dawn

Hours before the dawn,
the stars still bright in the wide, dark sky,
the town birds roosting in trees and shrubs
began to chatter—
grackles, starlings, robins and sparrows—
for off to the north a train moaned
as it approached our prairie town,
moaning in commercial power and anxiety,
slowed slightly for the curve into town,
moaned again and rattled off south to Louisville.
The sky still dark,
the new day not even beginning to dim the other stars,
the birds were frightened.
but the town's folk slept on,
awakening after the day had dawned
and rising to the things the railroad had brought them.

The Uptight Jay

An uptight jay preached from an elm branch
on the virtues of private property
and claimed the tree as his.
Two grackles on a telephone pole chuckled.
Satisfied that the law had been promulgated
and that his order prevailed,
the jay leaped to a feeder box in a rose garden,
and scattered barley and oats to get the sunflower seeds.
Two mourning doves cooed and whurried into the elm,
promenaded a branch above a swaying wren house,
cooed and whurried off again.
A downy woodpecker dug elm beetle larvae,
leaving the holes for the sapsuckers later to come.
Sparrows and more sparrows came
from their ragbag nests
in clothesline poles and garage eaves
to gossip and eat the mullet disdained by the noisy jay.
A robin pecked at the crusty earth,
then flew to the elm and proclaimed
his love song of territorial possession.
The jay challenged the robin, remained imperious,
lectured the sparrows eating the grounded grain
as a gang of starlings warmed themselves
around a chimney pot.
The sparrows ate and gossiped.
The starlings whistled.
Law and order and private property were life,
the jay declared.
At the tip of the elm, on a red-budded branch
a cardinal sang his phweet-phweet-phweet song.

Nighthawks, 2015, Homage to Edward Hopper, **photo by John D. Groppe**

The Nighthawks

In the morning retirees gather here
in this clean, well lit place,
needing each other's jokes
and memories more than the coffee.
At noon, workers come
for a quick lunch,
not for banter and memories.
After sunset come the nighthawks.
They sit apart, each to his own thoughts
of losses and what remains of hope.
The counter clerks,
busy at the drive up window,
leave them to their coffee
and will not notice that they have gone.

Instincts of Grace

The ball came toward me, a one bouncer,
and I bent slightly,
reaching almost without looking,
knowing the glove would meet the ball
just as it bounced,
still knowing that move after thirty-five years,
knowing it, following it and feeling the runner
so that I could throw to my brother at first
or Gillen at second to start the double play,
but today there was no runner—
only my son at bat
and me pitching in a field
far from the Bronx parking lot
where we had played as boys.

My brother—Gillen, Kenny, Mahon—
and all the companions of my youth, I trust,
can still make a sure handed catch
and have all the instincts of grace
we learned as boys.

Earth and Rain

The earth knew it before we did,
even before the birds,
and rose to join the rain.
Swifts, surprised by the soaring soil,
sortied as ground bound as sparrows.
Then we felt the wind and its promise.
Our desire had been buried deep within civilities
like an African plant nurtured in a city flat
without knowing the torrent
that had spawned its gentle purple.
The earth swirled, the rain fell, the birds fled.
Even then we hesitated,
sitting apart, laughing, our faces turned to the wind.
The honest invitation remained,
and we rose to dance with the earth and rain.

More You Than Me

You hand her to me, our child, my gift to you.
"She's yours too," you said.
She is more you than me.
Riding within you wherever you went,
feeding through you,
your breath, her breath
your blood surging through her,
her heart surging it back,
your voice, her voice—
she was more intimate with you
than I can ever be.
Still, she embraces me as you do,
and her own blood surging from her heart,
she grows into her own voice.
We smile at her—your gift to me—
and she embraces us with her own smile.

Community, acrylic by Adam Vanderwielen

On Adam Vanderwielen's *Community*

As if seen from the sky,
the little houses become
a kaleidoscope of dancers,
each community dancing
like Polish girls in billowing skirts
and colorful blouses
and young men in white shirts—
their shoulders firm,
their backs straight,
their black caps atilt—
all hand in hand
joyfully going round
in celebration of some ancient rite,
spring arriving, new loves burgeoning,
families extending—
each village in its own colors
dancing to its own joy
yet celebrating also
the joys and hopes
of all the other villages,
and even at this height
we hear the music—
the fiddles and flutes,
and horns and drums—
directing the dancers' feet
and we join the whirling circles.

The Word That Comes

We see nothing that has not been seen before
for in seeing, the word is one with the vision
so that we see with our ears,
hearing and releasing the word that is in us,
the word that has come to us from being among people,
and, if that vision strikes us speechless,
and we await the word in hope and wonder,
the word that comes still comes to us
from our father tongue and our mother tongue,
from the days and years and centuries of speech,
of gentle speech and violent speech,
of happy, sad and quiet speech.
The word that comes arises
out of the words of peoples,
out of the past, with word giving birth to word,
every new vision being found
within the ancient tongues,
analogy ramified,
metaphor bearing forth metaphor
in which itself is reborn,
all derived from that first word, that first vision—
what a morning that must have been.

Word Winger: A Self Portrait

Formalist, former of forms
bearer of patterns
silent singer, motionless dancer
winger of words, worder of wings
impatient with form,
hoper in patterns
parader, commander, leader and follower
opener of tongues, freer of pens
father of words, mother of poems
silent drummer.

About the Author

Photo by Jose Arteaga

John D. Groppe was born in Brooklyn, New York and raised in the Bronx. He attended Saint Luke's Elementary School and Cardinal Hayes High School. He received his undergraduate degree, a B.S. in Education, from the College of the City of New York (1954) and an M.A. in American Literature from Columbia University (1960). He served as a Rifle Platoon Leader and Company Executive Officer in the 3rd Infantry Division at Fort Benning, Georgia (1954-1956) and was discharged with the rank of First Lieutenant.

He taught at Villanova University as a Lecturer (1957-58), the University of Notre Dame as a Teaching Assistant (1958-60), at Indiana University-South Bend as a Lecturer (1960-62), and at Saint Joseph's College, Rensselaer, Indiana (1962-2003) and retired as Professor Emeritus of English. He was awarded Saint Joseph's College's Father Kaiser Faculty Scholar Award (1982) and Life Time Achievement Award (2003).

Since retirement he has been active in area arts organizations: The Prairie Writers Guild, The Prairie Arts Council, and The Jasper County Art League.

He is married to Rose Marie née Nigro formerly of Walsenburg, Colorado. They have five children and ten grandchildren.

www.ingramcontent.com/pod-product-compliance
Lightning Source LLC
Chambersburg PA
CBHW041528090426
42736CB00036B/234